I0149870

Advent And Lent In Narnia

A *"Fantastic"* Worship Series For All Ages

Rolf Svanoe

CSS Publishing Company
Lima, Ohio

ADVENT AND LENT IN NARNIA

FIRST EDITION
Copyright © 2022
by CSS Publishing Co., Inc.

Published by CSS Publishing Company, Inc., Lima, Ohio 45807. All rights reserved. No part of this publication may be reproduced in any manner whatsoever without the prior permission of the publisher, except in the case of brief quotations embodied in critical articles and reviews. Inquiries should be addressed to: CSS Publishing Company, Inc., Permissions Department, 5450 N. Dixie Highway, Lima, Ohio 45807.

Library of Congress Cataloging-in-Publication Data

Names: Svanoe, Rolf, author.
Title: Advent and Lent in Narnia : a "fantastic" worship series for all ages / Rolf Svanoe.
Description: Lima : CSS Publishing Company, Inc., [2022]
Identifiers: LCCN 2022041579 (print) | LCCN 2022041580 (ebook) | ISBN 9780788030925 (paperback) | ISBN 9780788030932 (adobe pdf)
Subjects: LCSH: Drama in public worship. | Drama in Christian education. |
  Lewis, C. S. (Clive Staples), 1898-1963. Lion, the witch, and the
  wardrobe. | Advent--Miscellanea. | Lent--Miscellanea.
Classification: LCC BV289 .S83 2022 (print) | LCC BV289 (ebook) | DDC 246/.72--dc23/eng/20221107
LC record available at https://lccn.loc.gov/2022041579
LC ebook record available at https://lccn.loc.gov/2022041580

For more information about CSS Publishing Company resources, visit our website at www.csspub.com, email us at csr@csspub.com, or call (800) 241-4056.

e-book:
ISBN-13: 978-0-7880-3093-2
ISBN-10: 0-7880-3093-0

ISBN-13: 978-0-7880-3092-5
ISBN-10: 0-7880-3092-2

PRINTED IN USA

Contents

Acknowledgments

The Lion, the Witch and the Wardrobe, part of the seven volume *Chronicles of Narnia* by C. S. Lewis, has been a work of enduring popularity among both children and adults. No doubt, much of that popularity is due to its symbolic representation of Christianity. The other part of that popularity is that they are just good and satisfying stories. During the last fifty-plus years I have known and loved these stories. Thank you to C. S. Lewis, who has written these stories beloved by millions of readers like me. They have filled our hearts and imaginations with much wonder and joy.

Thank you to the good people at Peace Lutheran in Sioux Falls, South Dakota, and Greenfield Lutheran in Harmony, Minnesota, who allowed me the space to develop these ideas and try them out in various Advent and Lenten seasons. It has been so rewarding to hear the giggles of children as they make their way through the wardrobe to enter the magical land of Narnia. This story has helped many to grow in faith and deepen their love for Jesus Christ.

Thank you, also, to my wife Kimberly, who took the time to read and edit the manuscript and add her thoughtful comments.

My hope is that this book may be used by churches to have a "fantastic" Advent or Lenten adventure and grow in faith and love for what God has done for us in Jesus Christ.

"Aslan is on the move!"

Rolf Svanoe

September, 2020 – Decorah, Iowa

Chapter 1 — Why Fantasy?

Some people love fantasy books, and others just don't understand them. Some enjoy the escape fantasy brings them from the mundane details of life, while others consider it a huge waste of time. I'm guessing since you are reading this book, you love fantasy too, you are a leader in your church, and you are interested in sharing a fantasy series with your congregation.

I admit that I love fantasy! My first encounter with fantasy was reading *The Chronicles of Narnia* by C. S. Lewis. I devoured all seven books as quickly as I could. I was also old enough to make the connections to my life and Christian faith. I fell in love with Aslan and all the other characters of Narnia. I even had a map of Narnia hanging on my college dorm room wall. I found these books were not only entertaining, they gave me a deeper insight into who God is and what faith looks like. As an adult, I still love these books. They are like old friends that I like to visit again and again.

When it comes to church, some will consider the use of fantasy/fiction as a waste of time. *'Why spend time reading fiction when we could read the Bible?'* But that ignores the fact that there are many different kinds of literature found in the Bible. Some would consider apocalyptic writing a close cousin to fantasy. The parables told by Jesus don't describe historical people or events, yet their lessons are true. There are several examples of fiction included in the Bible. The fact that it is fiction does not change its status as inspired. *"All scripture is inspired by God and is useful for teaching, for reproof, for correction, and for training in righteousness"* (2 Timothy 3:16).

Truth can come in many forms, genres or media. The author, Ursula Le Guin, has written about fantasy, "Fantasy is true, of course. It isn't factual, but it is true."[1] There is truth in the fantasy world of Narnia that has spoken to millions of people over the years. The books have sold over 100 million copies and have been translated into 47 languages. *TIME* magazine included *The Lion, the Witch and the Wardrobe* in its "All-TIME 100 Novels" (best English novels from 1923-2005). Its enduring popularity shows that there is something meaningful and edifying in Narnia that can't be easily dismissed.

Some have claimed that fantasy literature is just an escape from this world. But others feel that the opposite is true. The creation of an alternate world is a safe place to examine our real world with new eyes. In an article in *The Atlantic*, author Lev Grossman talks about the impact that C. S. Lewis and the fantasy world of Narnia had on him. He learned that fantasy is not a place to escape your problems, but the perfect place to grapple with them.

> *The Lion, the Witch, and the Wardrobe* is a powerful illustration of why fantasy matters in the first place.... I bristle whenever fantasy is characterized as escapism. It's not a very accurate way to describe it; in fact, I think fantasy is a powerful tool for coming to an understanding of oneself. The magic trick here,

---

1 Ursula Le Guin, "This Fear of Dragons," in *The Thorny Paradise*: Writers on Writing for Children, ed. Edward Blishen (Middlesex: Penguin Books, 1975), 92.

the sleight of hand, is that when you pass through the portal, you re-encounter in the fantasy world the problems you thought you left behind in the real world. Edmund doesn't solve any of his grievances or personality disorders by going through the wardrobe. If anything, they're exacerbated and brought to a crisis by his experiences in Narnia. When you go to Narnia, your worries come with you. Narnia just becomes the place where you work them out and try to resolve them.

The whole modernist-realist tradition is about the self-observing the world around you — sensing how other it is, how alien it is, how different it is to what's going on inside you. In fantasy, that gets turned inside out. The landscape you inhabit is a mirror of what's inside you. The stuff inside can get out, and walk around, and take the form of places and people and things and magic. And once it's outside, then you can get at it. You can wrestle it, make friends with it, kill it, seduce it. Fantasy takes all those things from deep inside and puts them where you can see them, and then deal with them.[2]

Rather than being an escape from this world, fantasy can help us engage this world with a fresh perspective and insight.

I want to encourage you to use fantasy in your church. A journey into the world of Narnia can bring great blessing to your congregation, especially when used in the context of an Advent or Lenten worship series. Preachers can draw connections between

2 Lev Grossman, quoted in "Confronting Reality by Reading Fantasy" by Joe Fassler. *The Atlantic Magazine*, August 5, 2014.

Narnia and the biblical text in worship. A book study or Bible study on themes in the book can make further connections. Parents can read through the book at home with their children. Look on the internet for ways to buy the book in bulk, and then sell it or give it away to families who will attend the series. Schedule a special showing at your local movie theater of the movie version of the book. (Although, I admit to much preferring the book over the movie.) The use of fantasy can capture the imaginations of both children and adults, and having visited the land of Narnia, give them a deeper appreciation for what God has done for us in Jesus Christ.

Chapter 2 — The Problem With Metaphors: The Lion, The Sacrifice, And The War

When we read LWW as Christian metaphor, we need to first explore the function and limits of metaphors. I want to express some caution as we look at Lewis' use of metaphors, specifically his description of Aslan as a lion, his description of Aslan's sacrifice, and the metaphor of war.

Metaphors can be useful in helping us to understand our reality. Who hasn't listened to a sermon and struggled to understand the point the preacher was making, and then a sermon illustration or story opens up the meaning for us? Suddenly it makes sense. Metaphors can do that. The danger in using metaphors is that sometimes they limit our understanding of reality and create their own reality.

> Metaphors create their own reality while attempting to explain some part of the other reality — our origins, the origins of the earth, the mysteries of creation, the riddles of being. Nothing is more real than the fact that we mediate every reality with our metaphors, and often create realities more real and powerful than reality itself with them. It is tempting to say that metaphors are too much with

us and prevent us from having direct contact with reality. But that is absurd. Metaphors cannot be too much with us because we do not have any choice in the matter. They are intrinsic to symbol-using. The worst thing that can happen to you is not to know when you are dealing with metaphors, to mistake metaphors for reality, or fail to understand how reality is being mediated by a particular overt or covert metaphor. Metaphorical naiveté is not charming, as some other forms of naiveté are; it is dangerous, just as naïve verbal realism is.[3]

It is important that when we use metaphors, we read and explain them carefully, and that we communicate clearly not to confuse the symbol with reality itself.

The Lion. C. S. Lewis portrayed the central "Jesus figure" in LWW as a lion. Aslan is a beloved figure to anyone who has read the Narnia stories. But it is important that we take a little time to examine this metaphor for Jesus. A lion is often used to symbolize strength, authority, and dominance. In the gospels, Jesus was certainly portrayed that way in his teaching and miracles. His teaching as one with authority and his casting out demons communicates strength and power. However, a man hanging on a cross is certainly not a symbol of strength, authority, and dominance, at least not by the world's standards.

No doubt, Lewis borrowed the lion metaphor from scripture. The prophet John in Revelation 5:5 refers to a lion. *"See, the Lion of the tribe of Judah, the Root of David, has conquered...."* Many point to this passage of scripture

---

3 William H Rueckert, "Metaphor and Reality: A Meditation on Man, Nature and Words," 1982, qtd. In *KB Journal*, Vol. 2 Issue 2 Spring 2006. Accessed Sept 2, 2020 https://kbjournal.org/rueckert.

to find justification for a more muscular Messiah using traditional tools of power and force. However, a close reading of Revelation 5 gives no warrant for this. The prophet John drew a distinction between what he *heard* and what he *saw*. He heard about the lion and expected to see a symbol of great power. What he actually saw was a lamb, the opposite symbol on the animal food chain. What's more, the lamb was not just a lamb, but a lamb **"standing as if it had been slaughtered."** John didn't use the traditional word for lamb, but a diminutive word, something like "lamby" or "lambkins". It was as if John wanted to remove from the lamb metaphor everything that the world associated with power and conquering. The lamb was what all heaven adored in worship, not the conquering lion. The lamb was the focus of the book of Revelation. The lion did not make another appearance in the whole book. What the prophet John was doing with this metaphor is redefining the true nature of power, not as brute force, but as suffering love. "The paradox resulting from the dialectical relationship between what John heard (militant lion) and what he saw (slaughtered lamb) powerfully proclaimed that God's victory, God's conquest, is achieved only through redemptive love, a love willing to suffer if need be."[4] In redefining power that way, John was showing God's power and strength demonstrated in Jesus' death and resurrection. The lamb's nonviolence was what conquered in the end. If we are going to use the Aslan Lion metaphor, we will need to carefully explain it to our congregations. The metaphor of Lion can easily overpower the reality it points to and confuse the real meaning of scripture.

The Sacrifice. Aslan's sacrifice was the central metaphor in *The Lion, the Witch, and the Wardrobe* (LWW).

4 Ronald L. Farmer, *Revelation*, ed. Russell Pregeant and David J. Lull. Chalice Commentaries for Today (St. Louis, MO: Chalice Press, 2005), 64.

Even the casual reader of the book will be able to make a connection between Aslan's sacrifice and Jesus' death on the cross. Lewis' use of the terms "Deep Magic From the Dawn of Time" and "Deeper Magic From Before the Dawn of Time" are both helpful metaphors for us to understand what happened in Jesus' death and resurrection. But in the end, they are just metaphors. The metaphors themselves do not contain or capture the reality of what happened on the cross.

What did happen on the cross? Why did Jesus have to die? Did Jesus have to die? Christians have been trying to answer these questions for millennia. Any parent has struggled to answer the question asked by their children during Holy Week, "If Jesus died on the cross, why do they call Good Friday good?" How we answer that question matters.

In his book, "Making Sense of the Cross," author David Lose examined the various ways the church has tried to answer this question over the years.

> These are important questions, not only because the cross and resurrection stand at the center of the New Testament's story of Jesus, but also because the way we understand the cross very much shapes the way we regard God. Depending on who you listen to, the cross may signify God's anger at human sin, God's grief at human waywardness, or God's plea for us to return to right relationship. Further, more than one thoughtful Christian has asked why the cross was necessary in the first place, or even whether it was necessary. Behind these questions lies a darker one: what kind of God would require such a gruesome death to achieve redemption?[5]

5 David Lose, *Making Sense of the Cross* (Minneapolis: Augsburg Fortress, 2011) p.2.

Did God cause or require Jesus' death? What kind of God would do that? We need to think deeply about the metaphors we use to explain the cross, because they reflect directly on how we think about God and God's character.

Not only does our understanding of the cross impact our understanding of who God is, but it impacts the understanding of our mission as Christians. Just consider the way in which the symbol of the cross has been used and appropriated throughout the years. The Emperor Constantine used the symbol of the cross for military conquest. The cross has been used to ward off evil spirits or as a good luck charm. Many wear the cross around their necks, or as a tattoo. I don't think this is what Jesus had in mind when he said, "If any want to become my followers, let them deny themselves and take up their cross and follow me" (Matthew 16:24).

In his book, *Mere Christianity*, C. S. Lewis wrote about his understanding of Christ's death and resurrection. He was careful to separate the reality from theories trying to explain it.

> Now, before I became a Christian, I was under the impression that the first thing Christians had to believe was one particular theory as to what the point of this dying was. According to that theory God wanted to punish men for having deserted and joined the Great Rebel, but Christ volunteered to be punished instead, and so God let us off. Now I admit that even this theory does not seem to me quite so immoral and so silly as it used to; but that is not the point I want to make. What I came to see later on was that neither this theory nor any other is Christianity. The central Christian belief is that Christ's death has somehow

put us right with God and given us a fresh start. Theories as to how it did this are another matter. A good many different theories have been held as to how it works; what all Christians are agreed on is that it does work... Theories about Christ's death are not Christianity: they are explanations about how it works...no explanation will ever be quite adequate to the reality...We are told that Christ was killed for us, that His death has washed out our sins, and that by dying He disabled death itself. That is the formula. That is Christianity. That is what has to be believed. Any theories we build up as to how Christ's death did all this are, in my view, quite secondary: mere plans of diagrams to be left alone if they do not help us, and, even if they do help us, not to be confused with the thing itself.[6]

During the last 2,000 years, the church has struggled to find language to understand and explain just what happened on the cross. David Lose explained the four principal metaphors the church has developed to understand Christ's death and resurrection:
- Ransom and Victory
- Substitution, Satisfaction, and Sacrifice
- Example and Encouragement
- Event and Experience

Lose examined each metaphor and evaluated its strengths and weaknesses. What commends each metaphor to us? What difficulties do each present? He applied four questions to each metaphor: What's broken? How does God fix this in Jesus? What does

6   Clive Staples Lewis, *Mere Christianity* (New York: MacMillan Pub. Co., 1952) p. 53-56.

this say about God? And what does this say about our life in the world? In the fourth and final metaphor, Lose ended by saying that the cross was not a theory to understand as much as it was a reality to be experienced.

> [T]he cross and resurrection aren't just theories but actual events, experiences we have in the presence of the living and loving God... Once you know yourself to be a person that God loves this much then your whole outlook on life changes...Free to be the people God created us to be...Free to love, forgive, and care for others because we've been loved, forgiven, and taken care of. Free to model our lives after Jesus, standing up for the people left behind by the system that values law over the relationship, and free to remind everyone we meet that God's kingdom is different...That's the freedom of living in light of the cross and resurrection not as a theory that tries to explain Jesus' life in light of a failed system, but instead helps us imagine a new system all together and, not only imagine it, but participate in it.[7]

The death and resurrection of Jesus Christ, then, is not so much something to understand in our heads as much as experienced in our hearts, where we also die and rise again each day. Perhaps this is the value of fantasy, that it helps us to encounter the death and resurrection of Jesus Christ, not just as theory but as story that changes us from within.

Let me give an example. A mother of a nine-year-old boy named Laurence wrote to C. S. Lewis, explaining

7 David Lose, *Making Sense of the Cross* (Minneapolis: Augsburg Fortress, 2011) p. 181-183.

that Laurence was concerned that he loved Aslan more than he loved Jesus. She received a reply from Lewis ten days later when he wrote:

> "Laurence can't really love Aslan more than Jesus, even if he feels that's what he is doing. For the things he loves Aslan for doing or saying are simply the things Jesus really did and said. So that when Laurence thinks he is loving Aslan, he is really loving Jesus, and perhaps loving him more than he ever did before." *(from C. S. Lewis, Letters to Children. p. 52-53)*

This is indeed the reason for a worship series like this, that in coming to love Aslan, our congregation will come to love Jesus even more.

As the preacher prepares this Narnia worship series, it would be worth some time exploring these metaphors about the meaning of the cross, especially during Lent. The preacher will want to come to some clarity how to talk about the cross, and how to relate it to the central metaphor in LWW.

The War. C. S. Lewis ended LWW with a battle between the armies of Aslan and the White Witch, between the forces of good and evil. The metaphor, no doubt, spoke powerfully to him since the setting of the story is England during World War II. Having read LWW several times, both as a child and as an adult, I never noticed the power of the battle metaphor as much as when I saw the movie version of the book. The movie portrayed the battle in graphic detail, as much as it can for a PG rating. In the final battle scene, Aslan gave a great roar and pounced on the witch. Their two eyes meet and then Aslan delivered the killing bite (thankfully not shown in the movie). It can be difficult to reconcile this metaphor with the God/man hanging on the cross, forgiving his executioners.

Battle is a metaphor for the struggle against evil that we all sense. But caution needs to be expressed. The metaphor is so powerful that it could be mistaken for reality. The battle metaphor too easily can become a real conflict between opposing forces that demonize and kill each other. The history of the church is certainly full of crusades and other examples of reading the battle metaphor in scripture literally. I have personally noticed that as little children watch the movie it is some of these exciting battle scenes they most enjoy. This needs careful explanation.

Battle is a prominent metaphor that is used by the prophet John in the book of Revelation. We read of an army of white-robed martyrs marching behind a rider on a white horse who has a sword, all the trappings of a traditional military metaphor. This is what led D. H. Lawrence to describe the book of Revelation as "the Judas of the New Testament," implying that it was a betrayal of the spirit and teaching of Jesus to love one's enemies.[8] However, a close and careful reading of Revelation will show that these metaphors are not to be interpreted literally. The sword is described as coming from Jesus' mouth, an obvious symbol that demonstrates that Jesus' word is powerful and can cut to the heart and separate truth from falsehood, and good from evil (Revelation 1:16; 19:15). God's truth is an essential weapon in the battle against evil, but care must be taken in using this metaphor.

Let me provide an example from church hymnody. Over the years the church has found that certain metaphors obscure our understanding of God and the church's mission. Because of that the church has rejected an overt use of the military metaphor to

8   D. H. Lawrence, *Apocalypse* (London: Heinemann, 1931).

refer to the spiritual struggle. The hymns "Onward Christian Soldiers" or "Stand Up, Stand Up for Jesus," have been rejected from many hymnals today because the power of the battle metaphor obscures the reality it is meant to portray. Too many children and adults have confused metaphor for reality and were ready to use traditional military tools for what they thought were righteous causes. It is important that we read our metaphors carefully and not confuse them for reality.

Chapter 3 — Setting The Stage

Worship leaders will want to give some thought to preparing for a Narnia series. You are inviting people to enter a magical world, the land of Narnia. Consider ways to spark imagination and foster a sense of wonderment, especially with children.

How will you prepare and decorate your sanctuary? Some things are especially important in engaging the story. You will need a wardrobe filled with coats. A wardrobe without a back on it is important because it allows the children to go through the wardrobe as if they were entering the land of Narnia. Since most wardrobes have backs on them, you may need to have someone in the congregation build you one. At the very least, you could cover a free-standing coat rack with some boards and a door to create the effect. The important thing is to invite the children to follow you through the wardrobe. They will have fun and you will see their excitement grow as their imaginations are being engaged.

Another item you will need is a lamppost. Go to your local building supply store and purchase a lamppost to use for the duration of the series. Make sure someone can create a base to stabilize it and ask someone to wire it so that you can turn the light on.

In the book, the first thing that the children see in entering Narnia is the lamppost. It is there that Lucy first meets Mr. Tumnus. The next thing you will need for your series is a someone to play the part of Mr. Tumnus, someone who can be a dramatic reader. In your church, after the children go through the wardrobe, Mr. Tumnus will meet them at the lamppost to welcome them and read them stories about Narnia. You will want to give some thought to a costume for Mr. Tumnus. Look at the Tumnus character in the movie and see if you can create a costume that is similar. Perhaps a pair of pants with animal fur, a tank top, red scarf, and a pair of faun ears would be enough. It doesn't have to be elaborate. You can also purchase a faun costume online.

Mr. Tumnus will welcome the children to Narnia. He will set the stage for the message by reading the relevant section from the book. He won't need to explain the reading. The sermon will do that. At the end of his time with the children, Mr. Tumnus will send them back through the wardrobe with the promise to meet them again next week for more stories about Narnia. Use the Mr. Tumnus scripts included in this book as a starting point. (If your church has projection capability, you may want to consider showing a clip from the movie that corresponds with the theme. However, I find that reading to children is a better way of engaging their imagination than watching a video.)

Above all, use your own creativity to engage your congregation with the story, and have fun. For example, in Lent 2, go online and order some real Turkish Delight. Get enough so everyone in the congregation has a chance to taste it. After the service they will be wondering if there is any left over.

These are suggestions for setting the stage for your series. You will surely come up with your own ideas to adapt the series to your own situation.

Pictures from "A Lenten Journey to Narnia 2020," Greenfield Lutheran Church, Harmony, Minnesota.

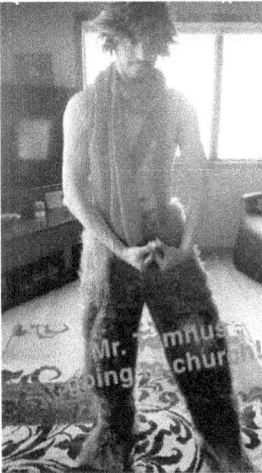

Chapter 4 — An Advent Journey To Narnia

The lectionary themes for the four Sundays in Advent are all quite similar in the three years of the Revised Common Lectionary. These Advent themes also fit well with the four Narnia sermons presented here. If your church has a tradition of holding midweek Advent services, this series will work nicely. But the series will also fit well into Sunday morning without having to leave the lectionary.

Advent is such a rich season of the church year, filled with powerful themes that are distinctly different from Lent. Christian educator John Westerhoff defined Advent as a time for hope, for dreaming of new possibilities, a time set aside to rethink the ways in which we choose to live our lives. Advent is a time of anticipation, of watching and waiting, and of transformation.[9] Advent is also the season for recovering lost dreams. In a world of despair and hopelessness, Advent comes each year with its reminder not to give up, but to believe and trust in God's promises of liberation. The discerning preacher will find that these themes fit well with Lewis' description of Narnia presented in LWW.

---

9 John Westerhoff, *A Pilgrim People: Learning Through the Church Year* (New York: Seabury Books, 2005)

Advent is my favorite season of the church year. But every year I am frustrated with the desire of the congregation to let Christmas creep into Advent. The demands of the choir programs or Sunday school programs will need to be navigated. But the four themes of this Narnia Advent series will richly reward any congregation that will allow Advent to be Advent.

Advent 1 — Always Winter, Never Christmas

Mr. Tumnus Script. Sons of Adam! Daughters of Eve! Welcome, welcome! I am so glad you are here in Narnia. My name is Tumnus and you can call me, Mr. Tumnus. I am a faun. Have any of you seen a faun before? You probably haven't unless you've been to Narnia before. I see that you came through the wardrobe. Yes, there are many ways into Narnia, but that way is the best. This is a special magical place full of fantastic tales and legends. I so love to share Narnia with visitors and tell them stories. Would you like to hear a story about Narnia?

This story is about a little girl, whose name was Lucy. She was the first human, the very first daughter of Eve to visit Narnia. I was the one to meet her and to introduce her to Narnia. Here is how Lucy came to Narnia. She came through the wardrobe — just like you did.

(Begin reading at Chapter One *"This must be a simply enormous wardrobe!"* Read to the end of the chapter.)

That's how we first met. I invited Lucy to my home and told her about Narnia and how in Narnia it was always winter and never Christmas. You wouldn't like that would you? Cold, dark, always winter. No Christmas to look forward to — that was Narnia, the world I lived in back then. That was before Aslan came. But that is another story. And if you come back next week, I promise I'll tell you more stories about Narnia. I can't wait to tell you about Aslan. But for now, back you go through the wardrobe. Your family is waiting for you. See you next week.

Sermon — Mark 13:24-37

I have loved Narnia for over forty years. I first read the *Chronicles of Narnia*, by C.S. Lewis, when I was in high school, and since then I have read all seven books several times. Each time I visit Narnia, these stories speak to me. Like any good story, we fall in love with the characters. But these stories give us a glimpse back into our own world. They have much to teach us about who we are and who God is.

C.S. Lewis did not start out to write a Christian story. Rather, he started with a magical world filled with talking animals. But his imagination was so thoroughly biblical that it worked its way into the story. Suppose there was such a world, and that world had problems like ours, and had someone in it like Jesus. What would Jesus look like? What would he do? C.S. Lewis said, he might look like a lion, named Aslan, who would give his life to save a boy in trouble. Here we have the central elements of our own Christian story — incarnation, atonement, death, and resurrection.

Over 100 million copies of the Narnia books have been sold in the last fifty years and been translated into 47 different languages. Someone has said that one of the best parts of being a parent is that you get to read these stories over again to your kids. I have fond memories of reading these stories to my children. I hope many of you with young children are doing that, and I'd love to hear how they react to the story. In May of 1955, the mother of a nine-year-old boy named Laurence wrote to C. S. Lewis, explaining that Laurence was concerned that he loved Aslan more than he loved

Jesus. She received a reply from Lewis ten days later when he wrote:

> "Laurence can't really love Aslan more than Jesus, even if he feels that's what he is doing. For the things he loves Aslan for doing or saying are simply the things Jesus really did and said. So that when Laurence thinks he is loving Aslan, he is really loving Jesus: and perhaps loving him more than he ever did before." *(from C. S. Lewis, Letters to Children. p. 52-53)*

In the third book of the *Chronicles of Narnia*, Aslan tells the children that they wouldn't be coming to Narnia anymore. They were sad, because they had come to love Aslan, and they think they shall never see him again. Aslan reassured them that they would meet him again, but in their own world.

> "But you shall meet me, dear one," said Aslan.
> "Are — are you there too, Sir?" said Edmund.
> "I am," said Aslan. "But there I have another name. You must learn to know me by that name. This was the very reason why you were brought to Narnia, that by knowing me here for a little, you may know me better there." *(from "Voyage of the Dawn Treader.")*

That is the reason we are having this series on Narnia. Our hope is that this story will help you to know Jesus Christ better and appreciate what he has done for you.

We are in the season of Advent, four weeks to help us get ready for Christmas. Waiting, hoping, and longing mark the season. As the daylight gets shorter and the snow and cold increases, it is nice to have something wonderful to fill our hearts with anticipation. Many of you are decorating your houses, buying gifts, and getting ready to celebrate the birth of Jesus with your family. But what if you lived in a world that had no Christmas to look forward to? What if there were no Spring coming, only an endless winter? We wouldn't like it. It would be depressing, even for those of us who love winter. That's the kind of world that C. S. Lewis presents to us in Narnia, where it is "always winter, never Christmas." It is not a happy, hopeful image, is it? In fact, it is rather depressing to think of an unending winter with nothing but more of the same to anticipate. Narnia was under the spell of a witch who had made it always winter and never Christmas. The people of Narnia longed for freedom and longed for an end to the witch's control.

One of the ways the witch maintained her control of the population was through a vast spy network. She had spies everywhere, even some of the trees were in her hire. People in Narnia didn't know who to trust. It reminds me of the time I was traveling with a group in the former East Germany. It was the summer of 1990, just after the wall came down. In Leipzig, our tour leader showed us the huge building that had housed the Stasi, the East German Secret Police. They employed thousands of people to spy on their neighbors, read their mail and listen to their phone conversations. Spies were everywhere, and for forty years they struck fear in the people of East Germany.

That's how it was in Narnia under the witch's control. There was one hope, however. There was a prophecy that said that when two sons of Adam and two daughters of Eve sat on the thrones of Narnia, the witch's reign would end. Aslan, the real King of Narnia, would return to restore peace and freedom to the land. That was the hope that filled the hearts of the people of Narnia in the midst of their endless winter.

That same kind of hope filled the hearts of God's people in the time of Jesus. They knew the prophecies that pointed to a Messiah who would come to rescue God's people, free them from their bondage and restore peace and justice. Those prophecies sustained them in the long time of waiting when it seemed like "always winter and never Christmas."

In our gospel reading today, Jesus reminds us of this hope and that he will come again someday — *"the Son of Man coming in clouds with great power and glory."* (13:26) He reminds us that as we wait, we need to be watchful and ready. *"But about that day or hour no one knows, neither the angels in heaven, nor the Son, but only the Father. Beware, keep alert; for you do not know when the time will come."* (13:32-33) Jesus sounds a bit like a coach trying to encourage his team during half-time, even though the game seems hopeless and lost.

Someone has said that Advent is a season for recovering lost dreams. It is a season to be reminded not to give up, but to reconnect to the hope that God will indeed come to our world and into our lives with healing and justice.

I don't know how many times over the last few months I have heard people express fear and doubt about the future. "What is this world coming to?" they ask. A global pandemic, threatening climate change, a growing movement for racial justice and equality, not to mention the increasing polarization in our country, all of it makes us uneasy and fearful. But this is precisely why we need Advent. When our lives seem hopeless, we need to reconnect to the hope that God is bringing. We need to know that instead of unending winter, there is hope that Jesus is coming into our world, that he will show up in surprising ways to bring peace and healing.

Perhaps you are dealing with insurmountable problems in your life, things that never seem to change and never get fixed. Sometimes life can beat us down so much we feel like giving up. Always winter, never Christmas — and that is when we need Advent. We need Jesus encouraging us to hope, to focus on him and his power instead of our problems. That is when we will find him showing up in surprising ways and surprising places. Don't give up. Keep your hope alive because God is alive, and Jesus is coming *"with great power and glory."*

Advent 2 — Aslan Is On The Move

Mr. Tumnus Script. Welcome sons of Adam and daughters of Eve. I'm so glad to welcome you back to Narnia. This is truly a magical place and I love to tell stories of Narnia. Today I get to tell you about Aslan. That's the best story of all. But first, here's how the story starts. Peter, Edmund, Susan, and Lucy all came to Narnia through the wardrobe. They discovered that I had been arrested. They met Mr. Beaver who invited them to his home. And while they were there, Mr. and Mrs. Beaver told them about Aslan.

(Begin reading at chapter 8. Read until, "Safe? Who said anything about safe? 'Course he isn't safe. But he's good. He's the King I tell you.")

Do you think you'd like to meet Aslan? Or would you be afraid to face a lion? Well, Aslan is a good lion, and we here in Narnia all love him and owe him our lives. But that's another story. Will you come back again next week and share another story with me? Goodbye sons of Adam and daughters of Eve.

Sermon — Mark 1:1-8

It is December with its cold weather and long nights. Around here, the sun rises about 8:00 in the morning and sets about 5:00 in the evening. That gives us nine hours of daylight and fifteen hours of darkness. Now lest we complain too much, let me tell you about the residents of Kirkenes, Norway. Kirkenes is way up at the top of Norway, as far north as you can get on the continent of Europe. There the sun sets on November 27 and they won't see the direct rays of the sun again until January 15. That's seven whole weeks without seeing direct sunlight. Can you imagine seven whole weeks without seeing the sun? The Norwegians call it the *Mørketid*, or the "dark time." The lack of sunlight can cause depression, or seasonal affective disorder. For some people, this can be a real problem. The one thing that gives hope is knowing it won't last forever. After the winter solstice, the days begin to get longer. Those extra few minutes of sunlight each day are like good news for a sun-starved soul. The sun will return and on the summer solstice, Norway becomes the Land of the Midnight Sun, where the sun never sets.

The gospel of Mark begins with these words, *"The beginning of the good news of Jesus Christ, the Son of God."* To people living in darkness, this was a bold announcement that things were about to change. God is coming among us and the world is about to turn. Get ready! Prepare the way of the Lord! This was the message of good news proclaimed by John the Baptist. Something big is about to happen. Someone important is coming.

This is the image we can keep in mind as we read C. S. Lewis' wonderful book, *The Lion, the Witch, and the*

Wardrobe. In this children's fantasy story, Lewis brings us to the magical world of Narnia. Narnia was under the spell of the witch, the Queen of Narnia, who had made the land always winter, but never Christmas. It was her way of controlling Narnia and suppressing any revolt. The witch had spies everywhere that she used to maintain her control. The creatures of Narnia lived with little hope. They yearned for the day when they could be free of the witch's control. And the one ray of hope they had was the story of Aslan.

Four children entered into Narnia and there they encountered Mr. Beaver who told them about Aslan. Here is how Lewis described when the children first heard the name Aslan.

> [Mr. Beaver whispered] "They say Aslan is on the move — perhaps has already landed." And now a curious thing happened. None of the children knew who Aslan was any more than you do; but the moment the Beaver had spoken these words everyone felt quite different...At the name of Aslan each one of the children felt something jump in its inside... that strange feeling — like the first signs of spring, like good news, had come over them.[10]

Mr. Beaver went on to explain to the children who Aslan was.

> Aslan?" said Mr. Beaver. "Why, don't you know? He's the King. He's the Lord of the whole wood, but not often here, you understand. Never in my time or my father's time. But the word has reached us that he has come back. He is in Narnia at this moment.

10 C. S. Lewis, *The Lion, the Witch and the Wardrobe* (New York: Collier Books, 1970) p. 64

He'll settle the White Queen all right... No, no. He'll put all to rights as it says in an old rhyme in these parts:

Wrong will be right, when Aslan comes in sight. At the sound of his roar, sorrows will be no more,
When he bares his teeth, winter meets its death,
And when he shakes his mane, we shall have spring again.[11]

The situation the children encountered in Narnia was similar to that which we see in our gospel reading. Into a dark world of despair comes a ray of hope. It was not Aslan who was on the move, but Jesus, the Messiah. The Messiah was the one for whom God's people yearned, longed and prayed fervently. The Messiah would be the one to free them from their Roman oppressors. The announcement of Jesus' arrival was indeed good news. God's people needed to get ready. Prepare the way!

If someone important were coming to visit at your house, I imagine you would want to make some preparations. You'd certainly do some cleaning. If this person were really important, you might even do some remodeling. Or, what if you were getting ready for the wedding of one of your adult children? Would you go on a diet so you can fit into your clothes? Would you take a dance class? Important events often bring with them a sense of hope, anticipation, and expectation. Getting ready can mean making some big changes.

John the Baptist's message comes to us with excitement, hope, and expectation. And yet, his message often finds us in places of hopelessness and

11 *Ibid.* p. 74.

despair. Sometimes we are weary with the ugliness in the world. Some of us deal with chronic personal struggles we never seem to get over. There are the cries for racial justice and reform in our world, the struggle to bring people together in peace who come from different ethnic and religious backgrounds. We long for peace in our world and an end to seemingly unending conflicts. We worry about global pandemics and how to protect each other from the coronavirus. And over all that is the concern of our human impact on the creation and how to prevent disastrous climate changes. Sometimes these problems can seem insurmountable.

To us, today, John the Baptist comes with a message of encouragement. Don't give up your dreams for a better world. Messiah is coming. The world will change. Believe and hope in God again. We walk by faith not by sight. When our vision tells us that nothing will ever change, our faith tells us to prepare the way of the Lord. Jesus is on the move! That's how John wanted us to hear his message.

Jesus' mother, Mary, had a similar reaction to the announcement she would bear the Messiah. Her life was about to change. The whole world was about to turn. And what did she do? She broke out into song. Her song is called the Magnificat. There is a modern version of that song in our hymnal called, "The Canticle of the Turning." (These lyrics are under copyright and can't be reprinted without permission, but are easily found on the internet.)

Mary announced it. John the Baptist announced it. Mr. Beaver announced. Aslan is on the move! Messiah is coming! Get ready! Believe again. The world is about to turn. Don't despair. Trust in God. The world is about to turn.

Advent 3 — Father Christmas

Mr. Tumnus Script. Welcome! Welcome daughters of Eve and sons of Adam. Welcome back to Narnia. I hope you have had a good week. I understand in your world you are getting to celebrate Christmas. Well, today I want to tell you about Father Christmas and the time he came to Narnia. He brought presents! Here's the story. Edmund had been captured by the White Witch. The other three children knew that the witch would be coming for them. So, with Mr. and Mrs. Beaver they escaped to a hiding place. While they were hiding, they heard sleigh bells. They were afraid that the witch had found them. Mr. Beaver went to check and came back with some good news.

(Begin reading Chapter 10 — "It's all right," he was shouting. "Come out Mrs. Beaver. Come out, Sons and Daughters of Adam. It's all right. It isn't her." Read until, "and he and the reindeer and the sledge and all were out of sight before anyone realized that they had started.")

Father Christmas was amazing, wasn't he? Did you notice something about the gifts that he gave everyone? Each gift he gave wasn't a toy for them to play with, but something to be used to help others. For example, Lucy was given a bottle with juice that was so powerful just a few drops could heal any wound. Wow! I hope when you go to buy or make presents to give away, you remember Father Christmas.

Next week, I want to tell you one of my favorite stories in Narnia. That's the story when Aslan saved me after the witch had turned me to stone. Will you come back next week? See you then. Bye for now Sons of Adam and Daughters of Eve.

Sermon — John 1:6-8, 19-28

Excitement is building for Christmas. Have you been getting ready? We spend time buying presents, decorating our homes, baking special Christmas foods, and going to parties. Christmas is a special time of the year.

Christmas also makes a brief appearance in the book we have been looking at this Advent, *The Lion, the Witch and the Wardrobe* (LWW). In C. S. Lewis' fantasy land there is a special character whose name is Father Christmas. He rode in a sleigh pulled by reindeer and he handed out gifts to the four children from our world. He sounded a lot like Santa Claus. I suppose that C. S. Lewis wanted us to make that association. It is not coincidence that Father Christmas showed up at the same time as Aslan, who is the Jesus figure in the story. Father Christmas told us that the witch had kept him out of Narnia for a long time. Remember that in Narnia, it was always winter and never Christmas. But Aslan was on the move; Father Christmas had gotten into Narnia, and the witch's hold on the land was beginning to loosen.

In our gospel reading today, we learn of John the Baptist, who appeared at the same time as Jesus. "There was a man sent from God, whose name was John. He came as a witness to testify to the light, so that all might believe through him...The true light, which enlightens everyone, was coming into the world." (1:6-9) Father Christmas and John the Baptist are similar in that they both announce the good news of the coming Savior. They both call people to prepare their hearts. They both are signs that the world is about to change. "Make straight the way of the Lord." Jesus is coming to renew our hearts, and to renew our world. Are you ready?

I remember one time stopping to visit at the home of one of my members. I didn't call ahead of time or make an appointment. I just showed up at the door. When she came to the door, the look on her face said it all. She was upset that I hadn't called to give her a warning. Perhaps she was worried that her house was too messy to present to her pastor. She did not invite me in. I never made that mistake again.

John announced the good news. Jesus is coming. *"The true light which enlightens everyone was coming into the world."* If someone was coming to visit at your home, what would they find? Would you want them going through every room? Would you want them browsing in all your drawers and closets, revealing all the secrets you have hidden there? Yet that is what the true light reveals. The ways into our heart are often dark and twisted. We don't like it when someone exposes the secrets hidden there. But Jesus comes to reveal the truth about us. We are all broken and flawed, imperfect people, who would sometimes rather hide in the darkness instead of being seen in the light. The light exposes the truth about who we are, but also exposes the truth about God. In Jesus Christ, God has come among us to forgive sins, and to show us that we are loved freely and unconditionally. That truth has the power to change our lives and to change our world. John the Baptist is telling us to get ready for some big changes coming to our world.

When Father Christmas showed up, he gave the children gifts. He called them "tools," not toys. To Peter, he gave a shield and a sword. To Susan, he gave a bow, arrows, and also a horn that would summon help when blown. To Lucy, he gave a bottle with a juice that could cure any wound with just a few drops. These gifts sound like weapons for battle. But Father

Christmas called them tools. A tool is something we use to help us do our job, to help us fulfill our mission. Peter's sword perhaps stands for God's word and the truth it reveals. Susan's horn might represent prayer. Lucy's bottle could symbolize the healing ministry of the church. The gifts that Father Christmas gave the children were not for their enjoyment. These gifts were to help them to do their jobs, to fulfill their mission. And just like that, the Holy Spirit gives each of us gifts, not for our enjoyment, but to use to fulfill our mission to bring God's healing to the world. In many ways this sounds similar to the language used to describe the mission given us in baptism:

> To live among God's faithful people,
>
> To hear the word of God and share in the Lord's supper,
>
> To proclaim the good news of God in Christ through word and deed,
>
> To serve all people, following the example of Jesus,
>
> And to strive for justice and peace in all the earth.[12]

Make straight the way of the Lord. Jesus is here. The world is changing. Let's use the time and the gifts God has given us to welcome that change into our hearts and our world.

Advent 4 — The Lion's Breath

Mr Tumnus Script. Welcome, welcome, sons of Adam and daughters of Eve. We meet again. I have

12 *Evangelical Lutheran Worship* (Minneapolis: Augsburg Fortress, 2006) p. 236.

really enjoyed our times together, telling stories of Narnia. Today I get to tell you my favorite story, because it is the story of what Aslan did for me.

Just like I am welcoming you here to Narnia, I was the first one to welcome Lucy to Narnia when she first came. But when the witch heard what I had done, she arrested me, put me in prison and turned me to stone. It was awful. Can you imagine what that was like? But then Aslan came to the witch's castle and freed all the creatures like me that she had turned to stone. But let me read it to you.

(Read from the start of Chapter 16 to "and the blue hills beyond that and beyond them the sky.")

Can you believe it? Aslan brought me back to life again. With his sweet breath he restored me. It was the best day of my life. I owe everything to Aslan. I love him with my whole heart.

Sons of Adam, daughters of Eve, don't you love Aslan too? I know that Aslan loves you, but I have heard that in your world Aslan goes by a different name. Do you know what that name is? I hope you get to know Aslan in your world and that you feel his sweet breath blowing on your heart.

This is our last time together, at least for now. Thank you for sharing these stories of Narnia with me. Do come again. You are always welcome here in Narnia.

Sermon — Luke 1:26-38

I know that some of you think our Christmas in Narnia series is pretty cool. There are others who think this is just a huge waste of time. Some of you love it and some of you just don't get it. For those of you who don't share a love of Narnia, I can only ask your patience with those of us who do. For millions of people around the world, this story is a window into

God's great love for us revealed in his Son, Jesus. That is our hope.

Our last theme in the series is The Lion's Breath. At the end of the book, Aslan, the great lion, sacrificed his life to save Edmund. He died to satisfy the Deep Magic. But then something happened. There was a Deeper Magic that raised Aslan from the dead, and death started to work backward. Raised from the dead, Aslan, with Lucy and Susan, headed to the witch's castle. The courtyard to the castle was filled with creatures the witch had turned into stone. There is an amazing scene in the story, where the children find that their friend, Mr. Tumnus, had also been turned into stone. Thinking that he was dead, Lucy began to cry. But Aslan did something very special. (https://www. youtube.com/watch?v=yp5AIy-6bwE) Aslan freed those who had been held captive in the witch's control. With his breath he brought back to life those held in bondage. It is a powerful image.

As I think about this theme, I can't help but hear echoes to this story in the great hymns of Advent. (in the public domain)

> O come, O come, Emmanuel, and ransom captive Israel,
> O come, strong Branch of Jesse, free your own from Satan's tyranny;
> Hark the glad sound! The Savior comes, the Savior promised long;
> He comes the pris'ners to release, in Satan's bondage held.
> The gates of brass before him burst, the iron fetters yield.

These hymns express the hope and longing in the season of Advent. C. S. Lewis has done the same thing in his story, *The Lion, the Witch and the Wardrobe*. Aslan has come behind enemy lines to free his people. Advent is a time of longing and yearning for a world free from sin and violence, sickness and death. The Messiah has come. He is risen from the dead. Death is defeated. God's reign is at hand. He comes to you and me to breathe new life into our unbelieving hearts. We feel his breath upon us, freeing us from sin's power and filling us with hope and new life.

I love this story of the Lion's breath bringing back to life the creatures the White Witch had turned to stone. This story reminded me of visiting the Accademia Museum in Florence, Italy. It is the home of Michelangelo's famous statue of David. To get to David, one has to go through a hall called the Gallery of Prisoners, filled with other Michelangelo statues. The interesting thing about these statues is that they are unfinished. Michelangelo either rejected them or ran out of time to complete them. What people have found so fascinating is that even unfinished, the statues speak powerfully of the human spirit struggling to free itself from the things that hold us back. These statues remind me of people I have known in the past, people who were struggling things that imprisoned them.

1. a woman struggling with poor self-image after a childhood history of abuse
2. a husband whose grief at losing his wife just won't let go
3. a friend whose depression robs his joy and will to live
4. people who have struggled with addictions or living with debt that is crushing them

What each one needs is the master's hand and the lion's breath to free them within. They need Emmanuel to bring the good news of God's unconditional love and grace to heal their hurts deep inside.

We are in the fourth Sunday of Advent, a Sunday devoted to Mary and the announcement of the angel that she would bear a child who would be the Messiah. This is a different kind of longing and yearning. It is a hopeful waiting for new life and new possibilities. The angel announced to Mary that she would bear a son, the Messiah. Mary felt the breath of the Spirit, and she said, "Yes." Was Mary excited? Yes! Was she scared? Yes! Did she wonder if she would be adequate to the task? Yes!

One of my all-time favorite Christmas songs is called "Breath of Heaven: Mary's Song." It expresses Mary's hopes and dreams, as well as her fears and prayer for help. The song was written by Amy Grant at a time when she was pregnant and could relate to Mary's situation. As I read the words aloud, I want you to imagine Mary herself singing them. (These lyrics are under copyright and can't be reprinted without permission, but are easily found on the internet.)

The breath of heaven has power in it. That breath can free the prisoner. That breath can bring new life and new possibilities. It happened with Mary. She said "Yes!" to God's plan. It can happen with you. The Lion's breath. The breath of heaven! That breath is a potent symbol of the freedom and new life God wants to bring into our lives and our world. This Christmas season, I hope you feel that breath blowing into your hearts with new power and possibilities.

Chapter 5 — A Lenten Journey To Narnia

Lent is one of the few times of the church year when pastors are looking for ideas for a midweek series to use with their congregations. It is one of the few times during the church year when they are not constrained by the lectionary. The invitation to enter the fantasy world of Narnia will not only give them a creative alternative, but actually help them to authentically enter into the spirit of the Lenten season.

Lent is a season when we look honestly at who we are and acknowledge our need for God's grace. We begin with an Ash Wednesday confession of our mortality. We name our sins, our brokenness, our lack of faith and the fears that paralyze us. Christian educator John Westerhoff has described Lent this way.

> Every Lent we face up to the struggle of acknowledging who we really are. We continue the battle with the principalities and powers in our lives and histories that prevent us — not entirely against our will — from actualizing our true identity. The stories told during Lent help us to face up to our temptations and every present threat of evil. They help us to face up to the ways in which we need to die and the narrow gate through which we

need to pass. They help us to face up to our blurred visions, misplaced loyalties, and wrongful desires. They help us face up to our blindness and the healing and nourishment we need. And they help us face up to the ways in which we are bound and trapped.[13]

Pastors will find that the themes from LWW that are chosen for this series will fit very nicely into this general description of Lent. The seductive power of the White Witch is a potent metaphor for discussing the struggle with the power of sin and death that we find in our hearts and in our world. Aslan's sacrifice and the Deeper Magic is powerful metaphor for exploring the meaning of Jesus' death and resurrection. Entering into the magical world of Narnia can help congregations to view Lent as more than just a season they are asked to give up something. They are invited on a "fantastic" journey to the world of Narnia.

Lent 1 — Ash Wednesday: Sons Of Adam, Daughters Of Eve

Mr. Tumnus Script. Hello, hello. Welcome Sons of Adam and Daughters of Eve. Welcome to Narnia. I'm Mr. Tumnus, a faun. The top half of me is like you and the bottom half like a goat. Now, you don't need to be afraid of me at all. I'm just glad that you have come to visit our land. Narnia is a magical place, where many of the animals talk. Why, even some of the birds and the trees can talk. And here we have nymphs and dryads and fauns and... Oh it is a wonderful place! Well, it would be except for one thing. It's always winter here. We are under the spell of the White Witch. But someday, Aslan will come to rescue us from the White

13 Westerhoff, *A Pilgrim People: Learning Through the Church Year*. p. 82

Witch. Aslan is the great lion, the son of the Emperor beyond the sea. Anyway, I'm getting ahead of myself. I'm sure that your world is just as wonderful, too. Sons of Adam and Daughters of Eve, I'm glad you're here and that I can share stories about Narnia with you. I'm going to read to you from our book. This is the story when the first person from your world comes into Narnia. Lucy is her name, and she hides in a wardrobe only to discover that it is a door into Narnia. The first person she meets in Narnia is me, Mr. Tumnus.

(Start reading at the beginning of chapter two and read to page 14, end of the second paragraph. *"...as if they had known one another all their lives."*)

Yes, we became good friends. Oh, I have so many more stories that I want to share with you. Will you come back again? Every Wednesday night I'll tell you another story about Narnia. Next week is one of my favorite stories, the story of Edmund and Turkish Delight. Turkish Delight is a candy, and we are going to have some real Turkish Delight here for everyone to taste. It will be so much fun. Now, it's time for you to go back to your world, back through the wardrobe. I'll see you next week.

Sermon — Genesis 3:1-19; Romans 5:12-17

I have loved Narnia for over forty years. I first read the *Chronicles of Narnia*, by C.S. Lewis when I was in high school, and since then I have read all seven books several times. Each time I visit Narnia, these stories speak to me. Like any good story, we fall in love with the characters. But these stories give us a glimpse back into our own world. They have much to teach us about who we are and who God is.

C.S. Lewis did not start out to write a Christian story. Rather, he started with a magical world filled with talking animals. But his imagination was so thoroughly biblical that it worked its way into the story. Suppose that world had all kinds of problems like ours, and had someone in it like Jesus. What would Jesus look like? What would he do? C.S. Lewis said he might look like a lion, named Aslan, who would give his life to save a boy in trouble.

Over 100 million copies of these books have been sold in the last fifty years and translated into 47 different languages. Someone has said that one of the best parts of being a parent is that you get to read these stories over again to your kids. I have fond memories of reading these stories to my children. I hope many of you with young children will do that, and I'd love to hear how they react to the story. In May of 1955, the mother of a nine-year-old boy named Laurence wrote to C. S. Lewis, explaining that Laurence was concerned that he loved Aslan more than he loved Jesus. She received a reply from Lewis ten days later when he wrote:

> "Laurence can't really love Aslan more than Jesus, even if he feels that's what he is doing. For the things he loves Aslan for doing or saying are simply the things Jesus really did and said. So that when Laurence thinks he is loving Aslan, he is really loving Jesus: and perhaps loving him more than he ever did before." (from C. S. Lewis, *Letters to Children*, p. 52-53)

In the third book of the *Chronicles of Narnia*, Aslan tells the children that they won't be coming to Narnia anymore. They are sad, because they have come to love Aslan, and they think they shall never see him again. Aslan reassured them that they would meet him again, but in their own world.

"But you shall meet me, dear one," said Aslan.

"Are — are you there too, sir?" said Edmund.

"I am," said Aslan. "But there I have another name. You must learn to know me by that name. This was the very reason why you were brought to Narnia, that by knowing me here for a little, you may know me better there." (from *Voyage of the Dawn Treader*, p. 216)

That is the reason we are having this series on Narnia. Our hope is that this story will help you to know Jesus Christ better and understand what he has done for you.

The first book of the *Chronicles of Narnia* is called *The Lion, the Witch, and the Wardrobe*. Four children from our world enter the world of Narnia accidentally through a magical wardrobe. There they meet a faun named Mr. Tumnus, who calls them "Sons of Adam and Daughters of Eve."

"Good evening, good evening," said the Faun. "Excuse me — but I don't want to be inquisitive — but should I be right in thinking that you are a Daughter of Eve?"

"My name's Lucy," said she, not quite understanding him.

"But you are — forgive me — you are what they call a girl?" asked the Faun.

"Of course I'm a girl," said Lucy.

"You are in fact human?"

"Of course I'm human," said Lucy, still a little puzzled.

"To be sure, to be sure," said the Faun. "How stupid of me! But I've never seen a Son of Adam or a Daughter of Eve before. I am delighted."

By calling the children Sons of Adam and Daughters of Eve, Lewis is referring to the creation story from Genesis 2 in which Adam and Eve are our first parents. Adam and Eve are symbols of all humanity. Adam and Eve are symbols of our common heritage as human beings. We are all created by God and not by chance or accident. We are all connected to God, to the earth and to each other. Adam and Eve represent the best and the worst in human beings. They represent our "age-old rebellion" to reject God's will for our lives in order to pursue our own desires.

Four children from this world entered the world of Narnia. In a sense, these four children represent us. And when we read their stories, we see a bit of ourselves in them, the good and the bad. We are not only connected to Adam and Eve, but in Narnia, we are connected to Peter and Susan, Edmund and Lucy. We too are Sons of Adam and Daughters of Eve.

On this Ash Wednesday, we are reminded of our connection to our first parents and to their rebellion. We are reminded that the consequence of that rebellion was death. To be a Son of Adam or a Daughter of Eve is to be reminded that someday, we will die. On this Ash Wednesday our foreheads are marked with the sign of the cross and we hear again those words spoken by God to our first parents, Adam and Eve. *"By the sweat of your face you shall eat bread until you return to the ground, for out of it you were taken; you are dust, and to dust you shall return."* (Genesis 3:19)

Ash Wednesday, however, is more than just a reminder of our mortality. In Romans 5, the Apostle Paul reminds us that if death came into the world through Adam and Eve, something else has come into the world through Jesus Christ.

> ...just as sin came into the world through one man, and death came through sin, and so death spread to all because all have sinned... For if many died through the one man's trespass, much more surely have the grace of God and the free gift in the grace of the one man, Jesus Christ, abounded for the many... Therefore just as one man's trespass led to condemnation for all, so one man's act of righteousness leads to justification and life for all. (5:12-18)

On this Ash Wednesday, we are reminded of God's great gift to us in Jesus Christ. Jesus came to this world to reveal God's love for us. Jesus came to show us a better way of life, so that in following him we may have abundant life. Jesus came to this world to free us from the power of sin and death and give us the promise of life eternal.

Today, we are reminded that we are not just Sons of Adam and Daughters of Eve. We are children of God, sealed by the Holy Spirit and marked with the cross of Christ forever. Amen.

Lent 2 — Turkish Delight

Mr Tumnus Script. Welcome, welcome Sons of Adam and Daughters of Eve. It is so good to see you back in Narnia again. Do you like my home? Do you like Narnia? I'm so excited that I get to share stories of Narnia with you. Today I'm going to read you the story of Turkish Delight. Edmund is one of four children who have come to Narnia, but Edmund isn't very nice to his siblings. In this story Edmund meets the White Witch, who tries to trick Edmund by giving him what he wants — Turkish Delight. It's a candy and I'm going to give you a taste of it right now. Do you like it? What does it taste like? *(You might want to ask some of the older children to help pass out pieces of Turkish Delight to the congregation so everyone can taste it.)* Well, let me read to you about a very special kind of Turkish Delight that Edmund ate.

(Start reading at the beginning of Chapter 4 and read to the end of the first paragraph on page 39, *"...I think I would like to make you the Prince someday, when you bring the others to visit me."*)

Poor Edmund. All he could think about was getting more of that Turkish Delight. But getting more and more of something isn't always good for us. If you ate a whole pail of ice cream, do you think it would be good for you? You might get sick. Edmund was eating candy given him by the White Witch. That really wasn't good for him. Not at all. Have you ever wanted to do something that you knew wasn't good for you? And then our Moms or Dads tell us we can't have it. They know it's not good for us or it is dangerous. They just want to protect us.

Well, next week I'm going to tell you about Aslan, the great Lion. If the White Witch is bad, well Aslan is good. Aslan is the most important being in Narnia. You are going to love Aslan. I hope you come back next week. And now it's time for you to return back to your world, back through the wardrobe. See you next week.

Sermon — Genesis 3:1-6; Romans 7:15-25

Our story tonight is about Turkish Delight. You heard Mr. Tumnus share the story with the children, how Edmund wandered into Narnia and met the White

Witch. She decided to tempt Edmund with something that he really liked — Turkish Delight.

How many of you have ever tasted Turkish Delight before tonight? A few years ago, I led a tour to Greece that included a three-day tour of the Greek Isles. We made one port of call in Turkey to view the ruins of Ephesus, some of the most fantastic ruins from the ancient Roman Empire. And while we were there everyone was trying to sell us Turkish Delight. You bought it in small boxes with different flavors. People were urging us to buy. "Four boxes of candy for $10.00. Okay, for you, a special deal. Five boxes for $10.00."

I don't know much about Turkish Delight. On the other hand, I know a lot about Turkish Delight, and so do you. You see the way C. S. Lewis uses Turkish Delight in the story, it is a symbol for whatever tempts us to want more and more. In the story, Edmund had wandered into Narnia by himself where he met the White Witch. Shivering in the cold, the witch offered Edmund hot chocolate and something to eat. It was Turkish Delight. But this Turkish Delight was enchanted, and makes you want to eat more and more of it. Here's how Lewis describes it:

> Each piece was sweet and light to the very center and Edmund had never tasted any-thing more delicious...and the more he ate, the more he wanted to eat...this was enchant-ed Turkish Delight and that anyone who had once tasted it would want more and more of it and would even, if they were allowed, go on eating it till they killed themselves.[14]

Turkish Delight is different for each one of us. It has many names in our world. Just one more drink,

14 C. S. Lewis, *The Lion, the Witch and the Wardrobe* (New York: Collier Books, 1970) p. 33.

one more joint or one more hit of cocaine or meth. Just one more trip to the casino, one more quarter in the slot machine. Just one more pornographic website, one more secret affair with a lover. Turkish Delight promises us so much, but in the end it never satisfies. We are left just wanting more.

> A pair of reformed drug addicts were fielding questions from a group of high school students and their parents and teachers. "Why did you start experimenting with drugs in the first place?" asked one of the kids. "Why did you keep it up? What made you want to move on to the harder stuff?" The two men exchanged knowing glances; then...one of them stepped up to the microphone and took a deep breath. "You really want to know?" he asked. "It was fun."[15]

It's not a new insight. This story is as old as Adam and Eve. The serpent tempted Eve. You remember the story.

> Now the serpent was more crafty than any other wild animal that the Lord God had made. He said to the woman, 'Did God say, "You shall not eat from any tree in the garden"?' The woman said to the serpent, 'We may eat of the fruit of the trees in the garden; but God said, "You shall not eat of the fruit of the tree that is in the middle of the garden, nor shall you touch it, or you shall die." ' But the serpent said to the woman, 'You will not die; for God knows that when

15 Kurt Bruner and Jim Ware, *Finding God In the Land of Narnia* (Tyndale House, 2005) p. 27.

you eat of it your eyes will be opened, and you will be like God, knowing good and evil.' So when the woman saw that the tree was good for food, and that it was a delight to the eyes, and that the tree was to be desired to make one wise, she took of its fruit and ate.... (Genesis 3:1-6).

The forbidden fruit was a "delight" to her eyes, and she wanted it. Are there things that are a delight to your eyes, but you know you shouldn't have?

Proverbs 9:17-18 says, "Stolen water is sweet, and bread eaten in secret is pleasant. But they do not know that the dead are there, that her guests are in the depths of Sheol." Like Turkish Delight, sin can be exciting and enticing. It promises us happiness, pleasure, and love. We start down that path and at first, it's fun. But because it never truly satisfies, we need more and more to get that same sweet feeling. Sin can become an obsession, like Turkish Delight was for Edmund. He wanted it so badly he was willing to betray his brother and sisters to the Witch. Temptation to sin is a slippery slope, a progressive path to death. Who doesn't know the tragic stories of people who have lost everything because of an addiction to drugs, alcohol, gambling, or sex? Some even lose their lives. This is when we have to trust that God gave us limits for a reason. God wants to protect us from making bad choices. If God says to us, "No!" even though we may want something badly, we have to trust that God knows what is best for us.

What is your Turkish Delight? Maybe it's not as glamorous as the ones I've named. Maybe it's a credit card and shopping until you're in debt up to your eyeballs. Maybe it's over eating, an appetite you can't control. Perhaps it's a bad relationship you just can't get yourself to leave. What is your Turkish Delight?

The apostle Paul knew the struggle against sin. In the book of Romans he wrote,

> I don't understand myself at all, for I really want to do what is right, but I don't do it. Instead, I do the very thing I hate. I know perfectly well that what I am doing is wrong... But I can't help myself, because it is sin inside me that makes me do these evil things... No matter which way I turn, I can't make myself do right. I want to, but I can't...Oh, what a miserable person I am! Who will free me from this life that is dominated by sin? Thank God! The answer is in Jesus Christ our Lord. (7:14-25)

Jesus can give us the strength to say "no" to temptation. When we are weak, he is strong. And when we give in to temptation, Jesus comes to us with forgiveness and grace to start over again.

In our baptism service we ask those being baptized three questions. Let's read together the three questions that all start with the words "Do you renounce..."

- "Do you renounce the devil and all the forces that defy God?"

- "Do you renounce the powers of this world that rebel against God?"

- "Do you renounce the ways of sin that draw you from God?"

Tonight, we say, "No!" to Turkish Delight, "No!" to the things that draw us away from God, and we say "Yes!" to God, "Yes!" to God's love and grace for us in

Jesus Christ, "Yes!" to following Jesus Christ each day of our lives.

Lent 3 — Aslan: Not Safe But Good

Mr Tumnus Script. Hello, Sons of Adam and Daughters of Eve. Welcome, welcome! It is so good to see you back in Narnia again. I'm so excited that I get to share stories of Narnia with you. Today I'm going to read you the story of Aslan, the great Lion. The story starts with Peter, Susan, and Lucy at Mr. and Mrs. Beaver's house. There they learn that Mr. Tumnus (that's me!) has been captured by the White Witch and turned into stone.

(Start at chapter 8 p. 78, "But Mr. Beaver," said Lucy... Read to page 80 and stop at "I'm longing to see him," said Peter, "even if I do feel frightened when it comes to the point.")

What do you think of Aslan? I've never met a lion without being just a little bit afraid. But Aslan is different. Aslan may not be safe, but he is good. He may be fierce, but he is always kind. One thing I know about Aslan is that he loves me and that I can trust him. I hope you get a chance to meet Aslan someday. Would you like that? Well next week I'm going to tell you about the White Witch and the spell she cast over Narnia making it always winter. But in this story Aslan comes to break the spell. I do so hope you will come back next week to hear this story. But for now, it's time to go back to your world, through the wardrobe. Bye. See you next week.

Sermon — Revelation 1:12-18.

It was 1969. Two young Australians had recently moved to London. They wandered into the department store to discover a zoo on the second floor. After hours of gazing at two small lion cubs in a cage, they decided to buy one, in the belief that they could give him a better life. They named him Christian. The two men cared for the lion cub and took him on walks. They played with him in the courtyard of a local church. But after a year, the cub had become too big and they decided to send him back to Kenya to return him to the wild. A year later, the two men decided to travel to Kenya to see if they could find their lion. They were warned that the lion had his own pride now. He was wild and likely wouldn't remember them. But the two men were undaunted and after many hours of looking, they finally found Christian. A video was made of the reunion that I want to show you. *(Youtube — Christian the lion reunion.)*

Put yourself in the place of those two men, standing there, seeing the lion coming toward you and picking up its pace. What would you be thinking and feeling at that point? This lion has been in the wild for a year. Is this lion going to remember me? Is this lion going to be safe? Am I about to die? Fortunately, the story has a happy ending. I'm glad it was a "Christian" lion!

In our story from *The Lion, the Witch, and the Wardrobe*, the four children from our world enter Narnia and learn about Aslan, the great Lion and true ruler of Narnia. Immediately the children are fearful and apprehensive about meeting Aslan.

> "Is he — quite safe? I shall feel rather nervous about meeting a lion."
> "That you will, dearie, and no mistake," said Mrs. Beaver; "if there's anyone who can appear before Aslan without their knees knocking, they're either braver than most or else just silly."
> "Then he isn't safe?" said Lucy.

"Safe?" said Mr. Beaver; "Who said anything about safe? Course he isn't safe. But he's good. He's the King, I tell you."[16]

This is the image that C. S. Lewis uses to describe Jesus. In the story, Aslan in Narnia is like Jesus in our world. What do you think he means when he implies that Jesus is not safe, but he is good? Let's take a look at these two ideas.

Not Safe. In our world, things are safe when we can control them. Think about fire? We use fire for all kinds of things that bring great benefit into our lives. But when fire is out of control, it destroys. Electricity runs our world, but when it gets out of control, it can kill. We all have natural gas in our homes to run our furnaces, but when it gets out of control, it can explode. You get the idea — something that is safe is something we can control. How many of you have pets at home? Our pets are tame, domesticated animals. We can train them and control them, mostly. But an animal that is wild is one we can't control. Lions generally are wild animals. We can't tame them; we can only cage them.

What does it mean that Aslan is not safe? What could it mean that Jesus is not safe? I think that by using this metaphor for Jesus, Lewis wants us to know that Jesus is not someone we can control. We can't manipulate Jesus with our prayers or gifts or promises. That's what a lot of religion is. "God, Let's make a deal. You do this for me, and I'll do that for you. Give me what I want, and I'll devote my life to serving you." You get the idea. But God will not be controlled or manipulated by us. We can only yield to God, submit to God and obey God.

In another part of the story Lewis said this:

16 C. S. Lewis, *The Lion, the Witch and the Wardrobe* (New York: Collier Books, 1970) p. 75.

People who have not been in Narnia sometimes think that a thing cannot be good and
terrible at the same time. If the children had
ever thought so, they were cured of it now.
For when they tried to look at Aslan's face,
they just caught a glimpse of the golden mane
and the great, royal, solemn, overwhelming
eyes; and then they found they couldn't look
at him and went all trembly.[17]

A similar thing happens in our reading from
Revelation 1. The prophet John saw a vision of Jesus in
all of his splendor and terrible majesty, and he fell at his
feet as though dead. Imagine the fear he experienced.
What's going to happen to him? And yet the first
thing that happened was that Jesus put his hand on
his shoulder and said to him, "Do not be afraid." This
Jesus is the one who "loves us and freed us from our
sins by his blood."

When confronted by Jesus, we quickly become
aware how small we are, how weak and broken. We
don't make deals with this Jesus. We have nothing
to offer him; we can only submit to him. And we can
only hope that when we do that, this wild Lion will
remember us and love us. Jesus makes no deals with
us; He doesn't promise to make our lives safe. He
simply calls us to follow him and take up our cross.
A cross doesn't sound very safe, does it? Jesus doesn't
promise us wealth or to make our lives comfortable.
He calls us to follow him. He gives us life.

But Good. The second word Lewis uses to describe
Aslan is the word, "Good!" When the children finally
met Aslan later in the story, he welcomed them and
called them by name. If they had any fears about

17 C. S. Lewis, *The Lion, the Witch and the Wardrobe* (New York: Collier Books, 1970)
p. 123.

meeting this lion, those fears melted away with that greeting.

We too, are reassured by Jesus' words of promise spoken to us at our baptism, calling us by name. In that promise we discover that we are not just known and remembered but loved beyond measure. This is a king whose love for us is even greater than our own faithlessness, even greater than our betrayal. His love led him to sacrifice his life for us. His death has brought an end to our enemies, to sin, death and the devil, through his own death on the cross.

The four children who met Aslan in Narnia learned that this fierce lion was indeed good, and that he loved them to the point of giving his life for them. And those four children on meeting Aslan, loved him with their whole hearts. We too have a God who loves us that much, a God who so loved that world that he gave his only son.

The video we saw at the beginning is a touching reunion of Christian the lion with his two former owners. This wild lion remembered and loved these two men. How rich for us Christians, to have a Savior, who knows us and loves us, and now calls us to follow him.

Lent 4 — The Spell Begins To Break

Mr Tumnus Script. Welcome back to Narnia, Sons of Adam and Daughters of Eve. I'm so glad to see you again and share with you another story about Narnia. Today's story is about the White Witch and the spell she cast over Narnia making it always winter. Can you imagine a world where it is always winter and never summer? Well that's the way it was in Narnia, that is until Aslan came to break the spell. So in our story,

Peter, Susan, and Lucy are heading off to meet Aslan, and they think the White Witch is after them. They have to hide in a cave where they fall asleep. When they wake up, something very special happens.

(Read from Chapter 10, The Spell Begins to Break, starting on page 105, "It seemed to Lucy only the next minute..." Read to page 107, "And Lucy felt running through her that deep shiver of gladness which you only get if you are being solemn and still.")

Wow! The Witch's power was broken by Aslan. Aslan is our hero in Narnia. We all love him. I know that you will love him too. But the best story about Aslan is what he did next. You won't want to miss the stories over the next two weeks, because it shows just how powerful and loving Aslan is. Thanks for coming today. Now it's time to go back to your world through the wardrobe. See you next week.

Sermon — Mark 1:14-15, 21-28, 32-34

The world has changed! There is little that is normal about life anymore. The Coronavirus has brought us to a global shutdown. People are hunkered down in their homes. Churches and schools have been canceled. We are learning new phrases like "social distancing" and "flatten the curve." But what is not new is God's love for us. The Bible tells us that Jesus Christ is the same today, yesterday and tomorrow. God has been with us in the past, and God will see us through this crisis and into the future. The psalmist reminds us, *"God is our refuge and strength, a very present help in trouble. Therefore we will not fear, though the earth be moved, and though the mountains shake in the depths of the sea.... The Lord of hosts is with us, the God of Jacob is our refuge."* (Psalm 46) God IS with us. God's love surrounds us each and every day, even in the midst of crisis. God reminds us to *"Be still and know that I am God."*

Dr. Michael Osterholm is the director of the Center for Infectious Disease Research and Policy at the University of Minnesota. He said that we need to view this pandemic not like a Minnesota blizzard that will last a couple of days and then we dig ourselves out. This is really a coronavirus winter we're entering, and we are in the first few days of that season. He believes that this will last well into the fall. Dr. Osterholm says that this will not be like the seasonal flu, where we just have to endure a short season of pain. He says that this is not like a blizzard; this is a winter, and until we have a vaccine, this virus is here to stay.

It is rather discouraging to think about a Corona-virus winter. We have all kinds of questions. When will this end? How will it end? How will I survive? How do we go through life fighting against an unseen enemy, a virus? When will this winter end? Will it ever end?

This is exactly the picture that C. S. Lewis paints for us in his story. In the land of Narnia, it is always winter. The land of Narnia was under the spell of the White Witch. Her magic was the power that kept Narnia covered in snow and ice. And the only hope that Narnians had that it would ever get better was that someday Aslan would return, and the Witch's power would be shattered. The ice would melt, and spring would come to Narnia.

This is the story Mr. Tumnus just told to the children. The four children from our world entered the land of Narnia, and there they encountered Father Christmas. His presence was a sign that the Witch's power was weakening. Father Christmas said to the children, "I've come at last...She has kept me out for a long time, but I have got in at last. Aslan is on the move. The Witch's magic is weakening." As the story developed, Spring did indeed come to Narnia, and the ice began to melt.

Aslan was on the move. His power was overcoming the Witch's grip on the land.

We see a similar situation in Mark's gospel. Jesus began his ministry announcing God's coming reign. *"The time is fulfilled, and the kingdom of God has come near. Repent and believe the good news."* (1:15) Miracles accompanied Jesus' teaching. The power of evil was overcome. *"That evening at sunset they brought to him all who were sick or possessed with demons. And the whole city was gathered around the door. And he cured many who were sick with various diseases and cast out many demons."* (1:32-34) Can you sense the excitement? Jesus' presence was something new. God's kingdom had arrived in Jesus to set people free from their prisons of body or spirit. When people are healed and reconciled with each other, evil loosens its grip on our lives. Jesus' ministry was to heal the sick and cast out demons, the powers of hatred and violence. His ministry was to shine the light of God's truth and justice into every cold and dark corner of our world. He came to rescue us from our sins of greed and prejudice so that we could experience God's fullness of life, abundant life.

Just like Jesus, Aslan was coming to bring warmth and freedom to the land of Narnia. He was coming to restore them to the way they were meant to be, the way they were created to be. He was coming to free the creatures of Narnia from the Witch's power, to bring an end to their winter, to bring hope and healing. And that's what happened in Narnia.

That is what has happened in our world with the coming of Jesus. Jesus brought the warmth of God's love and grace to free us from the power of sin. His forgiveness and compassion can warm our hearts and our relationships. You and I get to be a part of that movement. When we share God's love with others, we experience great blessing.

Have you ever heard of the world-famous Passion Play in Oberammergau, Germany? Every ten years, this small town in the foothills of the Alps puts on a passion play to tell the story of Jesus death and resurrection. In 1633, the region was threatened by the Bubonic Plague. The villagers promised that if God would spare them from the plague, they would perform a play. The death rate slowed; the village was spared. They kept their promise and the next year performed the play, and every ten years since then. The Oberammergau Passion Play has become world famous. Over 500,000 people attend. The irony this year is that the Coronavirus shut down the entire season. [The Passion Play resumed in 2022.]

Like the people of Oberammergau, we can be involved in sharing God's love with others. God's reign has come near to us in Jesus Christ. The spell is beginning to break.

Lent 5 — Deep Magic From The Dawn Of Time

Mr Tumnus Script. Sons of Adam and Daughters of Eve, welcome! Welcome back to Narnia. I so enjoy meeting you here and telling you stories about my home. Would you like to hear another story tonight? Well I am going to tell you the story of Edmund. Remember when Edmund ate the White Witch's Turkish Delight? Well Edmund kept thinking about it and wandered off to find the Witch's castle. The Witch made him a prisoner and tricked him into betraying his brother and sisters, Peter, Susan, and Lucy. Edmund was a traitor. He had done wrong. Edmund later was rescued, but the White Witch came demanding

Edmund's life. It was part of the Deep Magic that the Emperor had written into Narnia. It's like this: Have you ever broken one of your parent's rules and got caught? Maybe you got a time out, or grounded, or maybe you had something that you really enjoy taken away. That's what happened to Edmund, except that Edmund could be killed by the Witch because of the bad thing he had done. It's a scary story.

(Start on page 140. "A few minutes later the Witch herself walked out on to the top of the hill..." Read to the end of the chapter on page 144.)

Well, as I said, it is a scary part of the story, but I want you to know that it really does have a happy ending. But that's next week's story. I hope you come back next week because the story I'm going to tell you then is the most important and the best story ever for Narnia. And it's all about Aslan, the great lion. So, let's have you go back through the wardrobe, back to your world. See you next week. Bye.

Sermon — Romans 2:1-11

I'm sure some of you are still wondering why we are spending Lent on a book of children's fantasy? What does Narnia have to do with faith or our everyday lives? But stories have a power to touch us deeply. Some will read the book or see the movie and just enjoy a good story. But others will see a deeper meaning in the story. In Narnia, we discover something true about our own world. In Narnia, we meet Christ by another name. In Narnia, we fall in love with Aslan. In Narnia, joy is awakened. And when we return to our own world, we have a better understanding and deeper love for what Christ has done for us. I've seen it happen over and over again, as I've shared these stories with others. Some stories can capture our imagination and our heart.

A few years ago, parents were reading *The Lion, the Witch and the Wardrobe* to their young children. They finished the book and it was time for bed. They tucked their children into bed, said their prayers, and went downstairs. About a half hour later, they heard a terrible crashing noise upstairs and went running to see what was wrong. They found their five-year-old hitting the back of the closet with a baseball bat. "Johnny, what are you doing?" the parents asked. Little Johnny replied, "I just wanted to go to Narnia."[18] I want to go to Narnia, too. I want to see Aslan, to hug him and bury my face in his mane. My prayer is that you will too.

Tonight and next week, we come to the heart of the story. If the other themes we have looked at have been like salad or dessert (or Turkish Delight), tonight we get to the meat and potatoes. The two themes, "Deep Magic from the Dawn of Time" and "Deeper Magic From Before the Dawn of Time" represent the central theme of the story. In our world they represent the central metaphor of God's redeeming work in this world, the death and resurrection of Jesus Christ. You heard Mr. Tumnus read to the children. The Witch reminded Aslan of the Deep Magic from the Dawn of Time: "That every traitor belongs to me as my lawful prey and that for every treachery I have a right to kill." The law could not be broken or ignored. Indeed, if it was not satisfied, Narnia itself "will be overturned and perish in fire and water." It was the magic the Emperor put into the fabric of Narnia at its creation.

For us Christians, doesn't this sound familiar? At the very beginning of creation, God established certain limits for human beings. God warned Adam and Eve not to eat of the fruit of the tree of the knowledge of good and evil, *"for in the day you eat of it you shall surely*

18 Author unknown.

die." They disobeyed God and everything changed. They lost paradise, they lost their relationship with God, and they lost their lives. The Apostle Paul put it this way, "the wages of sin is death" (Romans 6:23). These laws are not arbitrary; they grow out of God's own nature and character. When we sin there is a consequence that cannot be ignored.

One of the images that figures prominently in Narnia is the Stone Table. The White Witch reminded Aslan that the Deep Magic was engraved into that very Stone Table. It is on the Stone Table that the laws of Deep Magic were satisfied. It was there that Edmund was to be executed for his treachery. Again, this all sounds strangely familiar, doesn't it? Instead of a table God inscribed the Law, the Ten Commandments, on two stone tablets given to Moses. The words 'table' and 'tablet' are close to each other, aren't they? In fact, one of the definitions of the word table is "system of laws or decrees; a code" (like the periodic table of elements.) Do you suppose Lewis had that in mind?

Have you ever served on a jury? I remember once listening to the prosecuting attorney make the case, and then the defense attorney. The prosecuting attorney impressed me. He reminded us that the law is the law, and that we cannot just ignore rules that we don't like. We are called to uphold the law. Without laws, a society will break down into anarchy. Everyone does whatever they want. It is no way to live. That is what Lewis meant when he said that if the Law is not satisfied, Narnia itself "will be overturned and perish in fire and water."

The Stone Table represents the Law, the commandments of God designed to keep the world running smoothly. It is the law that accuses and condemns the sinner. "All have sinned and fall short of the glory of God" (Romans 3:23). Like Edmund, we all stand guilty and condemned. The White Witch was right. She knew the Deep Magic. So did Aslan, and in order to save Edmund, he offered himself instead. The Deep Magic had to be satisfied, that was unavoidable. So, Aslan offered himself in place of Edmund, and the Witch killed Aslan instead on the Stone Table. Aslan died; Edmund lived. Jesus died for us; we live because of him.

Our theme next week is really the most important one in the story. The White Witch knew the Deep Magic from the Dawn of Time. But what she didn't know is that there exists a Deeper Magic from before the Dawn of Time, a magic that flows from the very heart of God. But that is the theme for next week.

Lent 6 — Deeper Magic From Before The Dawn Of Time

Mr Tumnus Script. Welcome, welcome, Sons of Adam and Daughters of Eve. I'm so glad you are here tonight for our final story from Narnia. I never get tired of telling stories of Narnia to anyone who will listen. Tonight's story is the best story of all of them. It is the story of how Aslan, the great lion, saved Edmund from the White Witch. When Aslan and the White Witch talked, they agreed that Aslan would give himself in exchange for Edmund. This freed Edmund, but left Aslan to be killed by the Witch. When she killed Aslan, Susan and Lucy were watching from a distance. After Aslan died, everyone left, except Susan and Lucy, who stayed the night watching over Aslan's dead body. But when the dawn came, something rather extraordinary happened.

(Start reading at page 160: "They walked to the eastern edge of the hill and looked down." Read until page 164, "the girls no longer felt in the least tired or hungry or thirsty.")

This story is the most wonderful and joyous of all. Aslan gave his life to free Edmund. But the Deeper Magic before the Dawn of Time said that when someone gave their life to save another, the Deep Magic would be broken. Aslan came back from the dead. And Susan and Lucy had such a wonderful time playing with Aslan and celebrating with him. Isn't that a great story? I think you have a story like that in your world, don't you? Isn't it a story about a man named Jesus? I think Pastor is going to tell you more about this Jesus. He is rather fond of telling that story, too. Thank you for spending this time with me in Narnia. It's time to go back to your world, back through the wardrobe. I do hope that someday you will visit again. But for now, I will say goodbye and wish you all the best, in the name of the great Lion himself, Aslan.

Sermon — Romans 3:21-26

Deep Magic from the Dawn of Time! Deeper Magic from Before the Dawn of Time! Maybe it seems a little strange to be talking about such things in the church. But these symbols in C. S. Lewis' fantasy world can give us a glimpse into our world. So let me ask — have you read the book? Have you seen the movie? I think that today's theme is perhaps the easiest to understand in connection with our Christian story. In Narnia, Aslan sacrificed himself to save Edmund. He gave his life just like Jesus gave his life for us.

Last week we talked about the Deep Magic that the Witch knew. The Deep Magic represents the Law in our world. It is the demand for justice. When you break the law in our world, justice is demanded, a penalty that must be paid. You might be fined or go to prison or both. In Narnia, Edmund broke the law by betraying his brother and sisters. The Deep Magic demanded his life as forfeit. Those demands were satisfied through an exchange. Aslan made a trade. He gave his life for Edmund's life. That was a trade the Witch gladly accepted. But what the Witch didn't know was that there was an older, Deeper Magic. Let me explain. In the story, after Lucy and Susan witnessed Aslan's death on the stone table, they gathered at his body and cried their eyes out. They had come to love Aslan. As dawn came and they began to leave, they heard "behind them a loud noise- a great cracking, deafening noise as if a giant had broken a giant's plate." The Stone Table had cracked in two and Aslan's body was gone. Suddenly, Aslan appeared, back from the dead. He explained that there was a Deeper Magic that the Witch knew nothing about. "If she could have looked a little further back, into the stillness and the darkness before time dawned, she would have read there a different incantation. She would have known that when a willing victim who had committed no treachery was killed in a traitor's stead, the Table would crack and Death itself would start working backward."[19] The Deep Magic was destroyed by an even Deeper Magic.

Let's look at it this way. The Deep Magic represents God's holiness and justice. It is real and it is important, something that cannot be ignored. The Deeper Magic represents God's love and mercy. That is what Aslan displayed in offering his life for Edmund. In the gospel of John Jesus tells us: "This is my commandment, that you love one another as I have loved you. No one has greater love than this, to lay down one's life for one's friends." (John 15:12-13) Jesus reveals God's love for us by giving his life for us on the cross. The Bible tells us that God SO loved the world. It also tells us that

19 Lewis, *The Lion, the Witch and the Wardrobe* (New York: Collier Books, 1970) p. 159.

God is love. God's holiness and justice are important, but even more important, even more central to God's character, is God's love. That is what Jesus came to reveal by dying for us on the cross. It is the Deeper Magic from Before the Dawn of Time.

In his book, *Written In Blood*, Robert Coleman told the story of a little boy whose sister needed a blood transfusion. The doctor explained that she had the same disease the boy had recovered from two years earlier. Her only chance for recovery was a transfusion from someone who had previously conquered the disease. Since the two children had the same rare blood type, the boy was the ideal donor. "Would you give your blood to Mary?" the doctor asked. Johnny hesitated. His lower lip started to tremble. Then he smiled and said, "Sure, for my sister." Soon the two children were wheeled into the hospital room — Mary, pale and thin; Johnny, robust and healthy. Neither spoke, but when their eyes met, Johnny grinned. As the nurse inserted the needle into his arm, Johnny's smile faded. He watched the blood flow through the tube. With the ordeal almost over, his voice, slightly shaky, broke the silence. "Doctor, when do I die?" Only then did the doctor realize why Johnny had hesitated, why his lip had trembled when he'd agreed to donate his blood. He had thought that giving his blood to his sister meant giving up his life. And he was willing to die for his sister.[20]

Is there someone you would be willing to die for? Is there anyone you love that much? Do you know anyone who loves you enough to die for you? Jesus loves you and did die for you, and in his death and resurrection he revealed to us the depths of God's love for us. As Saint Paul wrote in Romans 3, **"Since all have sinned and fall short of the glory of God;**

20 Robert Coleman, *Written in Blood* (Grand Rapids, F. H. Revell, 1972)

they are now justified by his grace as a gift, through the redemption that is in Christ Jesus, whom God put forward as a sacrifice of atonement by his blood, effective through faith."

The Deeper Magic that Aslan referred to was something the Witch could never understand. She ruled the world through power, fear, and intimidation. She knew nothing about love or grace. What the Deeper Magic revealed and what Jesus' death and resurrection reveal is that love is the most powerful force in the universe. God's love revealed in Jesus has the power to change our hearts, and the power to change our world. And maybe, just maybe, we have a better chance at understanding the incredible love God has for us because someone wrote a story about a lion, a witch, a wardrobe, and a land called Narnia.

Afterword

C. S. Lewis has impacted the lives of millions of people around the world. In 2014, my wife and I had the opportunity to visit Oxford, England. We had lunch at the Eagle and Child Pub, where Lewis and his Inklings friends spent much time enjoying a pint and exchanging ideas. We also visited the home where Lewis lived, and the church where he worshiped. Lewis died the same day that President Kennedy was assassinated, an event that overshadowed Lewis' death and the tributes that normally would have poured in from around the world. It was moving to visit his grave and to say, "Well done, good and faithful servant."

www.ingramcontent.com/pod-product-compliance
Lightning Source LLC
LaVergne TN
LVHW011412080426
835511LV00005B/507